The Death to Glory Ratio

Part 2

Find books by
Alonzo Triplin
use link below
amazon.com/author/apostlezo

By Alonzo Triplin

ISBN: 978-1-7372504-3-2

Table of Contents

Chapter 1

Will a man rob God?

Malachi 3: 8- 9

8) Will a man rob God? Yet ye have robbed me, But ye say, Wherein have we robbed thee? In tithes and offerings.

9) Ye are cursed with a curse: for ye have robbed me, ...

Will a man rob God? In order to gain clear understanding of this question, let us first gather the definition of the word "rob" in the context in which it's being used.

rob – to deprive of something due, expected, or desired.

Now that we have one of the definitions of the word "rob" listed, the one most relative to the usage of rob in this verse, now let's plug the definition into the verses.

Malachi 3: 8- 9

8) Will a man deprive God of something he's due, expects or desires, But you say, Wherein have we deprived thee (God) of what's due, expected or desired? In tithes and offerings.

9) Ye are cursed with a curse : for you have deprived me of what is due, expected or desired to me,…..

In the past 20 years many have taught and proclaimed financial prosperity teachings, centered around these verses found in Malachi chapter 3 as well as other such promises found throughout Bible scriptures. The multitude of teachings I heard emphasized that we have robbed God out of financial tithes and financial offerings. I consistently heard offer to the church ten percent of your financial income to represent your tithes and anything financial given over that is considered financial offering.

Just the other day God revealed to me that he was not only referencing financial offerings that he has been robbed of and that the curse that abides is due to lack of offerings far greater than merely financial.

In The Death to Glory Ratio Part 1, I illustrated repeatedly how those early men of God had a mindset to offer death offerings and otherwise, when desiring to come into fellowship with or seek deliverance from God. I pointed out that God is not a respecter of persons but scripture definitely declared that he was a respecter of offering.

Genesis 4: 4 -5

4) ......And the Lord had respect unto Abel and to his offering

5) But unto Cain and to his offering he had not respect,

So let's offer a bit of a summary of the things I've covered so far.

The lack of offering is a part of what God considers robbing him and causes a curse to abide. On the other hand, making offering that pleases God such as Abel did garners respect from God, causing God to respect and be pleased with the offering and whom it was made by.

Psalm 96:8

.....Bring an offering, and come into his courts.

This portion of Psalm 96:8 is a verse that confirms what I was saying to open this chapter, that the cursed state God speaks of in Malachi 3:9 was not due to just the lack of financial tithes and financial offering. This is evident here in Psalms 96:8 because financial material has use or place in God's courts or presence, but there are other offerings found in scripture that do and that garner the respect and presence of God.

I hope that right away the information that I've shared so far has grabbed your attention as it did mine when God shed new light. Journey on with me as I expound further into the teaching.

Chapter 2

Developing an offering mindset

Romans 12: 1-2

1) I beseech you therefore, brethren, by the mercies of God, that ye present your bodies a living sacrifice, holy, acceptable unto God, which is your reasonable service.

2) And be not conformed to this world: but be ye transformed by the renewing of the mind...

We see here in Romans chapter 12 verse 1 that he beseeches us to present our bodies living sacrifice, which can also be interpreted as a living offering. In verse 2 he then tells us to be not conformed to this world but to be transformed by the renewing of our minds.

One of my main objectives in writing this book is to transform believers who don't embrace an offering mindset, that they might develop one. To do this I will highlight its importance to God and the body of Christ.

Philippians 3:10

10) That I might know him, and the power of his resurrection, and the fellowship of his sufferings, being made conformable unto his death;

Romans 12:2 tells us to be not conformed to this world and here in Philippians 3:10 we are told to be conformed unto his (Christ's) death.

Scriptures such as these can be very thought provoking and create a need for diligent study and research for further clarity and understanding.

1st Peter 1:11

11) Searching what, or what manner of time the Spirit of Christ which was in them did signify, when it testified beforehand the sufferings of Christ, and the glory that should follow.

I want to focus attentions on the last portion of the verse here in 1st Peter 1:11 "the sufferings of Christ and the glory that should follow". Scripture teaches us that shortly after the death of Christ he was glorified. By these scriptural facts it is important for us to note that conforming ourselves to the death of Christ and fellowship of his sufferings by offering our bodies is always compensated by God with his Glory which is synonymous with his power.

2nd Corinthians 4:17

17) For our light affliction, which is but for a moment, worketh for us a far more exceeding and eternal weight of glory;

Let's break down this equations found here in 2nd Corinthians 4:17 which describes "light affliction" being exchanged for far more exceeding "weight of glory". Always remember that what we're offering God though it may seem difficult is light in comparison to the far more exceeding weight we receive in return. Not only is what we're offering God light, but it is also described here in 2nd Corinthians 4:17 as momentary in exchange for the eternal. Let us offer detailed summary of this equation. We are called to momentary light afflictions which we bare in forms such as obedience, sacrifice and offerings. In exchange for these, we then receive glory (God's power) that exceeds the light measurement of affliction that we initially offered. On top of all this, the light and momentary afflictions we are baring, gets exchanged for reward exceeding eternal. To exceed eternal means beyond time limitations, the rewards he is offering us for our momentary light afflictions will not only take effect in the limitless time space of eterntity but also rewards us in the time space of here and now.

The death to glory ratio parts 1 and now part 2 which you are currently reading show in great scriptural detail that God is a God of exchange and trade. Offering for Glory, seed for harvest, reaping for sowing etc. The death to glory ratio book projects pounder and provoke thought and experimentation as to how much offering equates to how much glory.

1st Corinthians 15: 31

31) I protest by your rejoicing which I have in Christ Jesus our Lord, I die daily.

We see abundant amounts of death offerings of sacrificial animals made on altars in the Old Testament. Scripture describes Jesus himself as the Lamb of

God who's death offering was made for the sins of the world. Philippians 3:10 tells us that we are to be made conformable to his death. Paul here in 1st Corinthians 15:31 states that he dies daily making it evident he isn't describing literal death because no person literally can die daily.

Let's take a closer look at the Apostle Paul's declaration that he "dies daily" and what resulted from it. Paul, daily afflicting himself as a death offering was endowed with a far more exceeding weight of God's glory on his life, to such a degree that he raised the dead, healed the sick, was used to write at least 13 of the 27 books of the New Testament etc. To sum it all up, a great ratio of glory was given him for the death offerings he sowed before God.

Considering all these factors from the life of Paul and many others throughout scripture who had the offering mindset, it is extremely wise of us to develop the offering mindset as well.

Chapter 3

Though I give my body to be burned

1st Corinthians 13: 3

3) And though I bestow all my goods to feed the poor, and though I give my body to be burned,....

Here in 1st Corinthians 13: 3 Paul describes two extreme sacrificial acts, one he describes literally and the other figuratively. In the verse he says though I bestow all my goods to feed the poor which he was referencing as something that literally can be done, then he mentions giving his body to be burned which is a figurative parallel and comparison to the burning of lambs and other sacrificial death offerings on the Old Testament altar.

"Though I give my body to be burned" in this term ,we again see the Apostle Paul figuratively referencing death offering of the body.

Biblically understood and interpreted Death offering is the greatest sacrificial offering a believer can give.

John 15: 13

13) Greater love hath no man than this, that a man lay down his life for his friends.

I used John 15: 13 to confirm where I previously mentioned , that laying down one's life in Biblically interpreted death offering and sacrifice is the greatest offering a believer can give. John 15: 13

makes it clear that there is no greater form of love.

Mark 9: 28 -29

28) And when he was come into the house, his disciples asked him privately, Why could not we cast him out?

29) And he said unto them, This kind can come forth by nothing, but by prayer and fasting.

Here in Mark chapter 9 scripture lists the story of a man seeking healing for his son. The man encounters Jesus himself and request healing and deliverance for his son, telling Jesus that he had asked the disciples to heal him previously but they were unable to. Jesus heals the man's son and that's where the story picks up in Mark 9: 28 - 29 with Jesus disciples asking him why they were unsuccessful in their attempt to heal the man's son. Jesus tells them that nothing prayer and fasting can get this done.

Some years ago the Lord revealed to me that fasting was a type of death and subsequently a type of death offering. To put it in the terms of Paul it is a giving of the body to be burned sacrificially on the divine altar. If you cross reference Mark 9: 28 -29 with Matthew 17: 20 -21 you will observe that in Matthew's example scripture describes the miraculous fete of speaking to and moving mountains in reference to healing a man's son and that these miracles could only occur by combining verbal commands with prayer and fasting.

We must understand that it is the anointing that destroys the yoke of infirmity and that fasting is a death offering that equates to loosing anointing Glory and power. " Death to Glory ratio" or in other words how much death offering equals how much yoke destroying Glory. How much of this(death offering) will I need to exchange for adequate supply of that(resurrection and miraculous level glory and power).

Experimenting with the figurative death offering of fasting is the only way to gain accuracy when counting up the cost exchange for mountain moving , miracles and miraculous healing.

Notes

Chapter 4

Offering and the cloud

2nd Chronicles 5: 6 ,13 , 14

6) Also king Solomon , and all the congregation of Israel that were assembled unto him before the ark , sacrificed sheep and oxen , which could not be told or numbered for multitude.

13) It came even to pass , as the trumpeters and singers were as one , to make one sound to be heard in praising and thanking the Lord; and when they lifted up their voice with the trumpets and cymbals and instruments of music , and praised the Lord , saying , For he is good: for his mercy endureth for ever: that then the house was filled with a cloud , even the house of the Lord;

14) So that the priests could not stand to minister by reason of the cloud: for the glory of the Lord had filled the house of God.

I've started this chapter off highlighting a scriptural chain of events. The first event I've highlighted is Solomon and the congregation sacrificing a death offering of innumerable sheep and oxen. The second event highlighted is a mass one accord praise with specific words of thanks and praise being offered up. The third and final event I listed is the cloud of God's glory filling the house of God.

Let us take a closer examination of exactly what has unfolded here that we might learn how to make these steps applicable in our assemblies in the house of God in today's times.

I've personally seen on television certain Christian conferences fill up a football stadium of sixty to eighty thousand believers in attendance. The Bible references believers as sheep very commonly (see John 10: 27) , the Bible also references stronger category of believers such as elders and higher as oxen (see 1st Timothy 5: 18). Both the sheep and oxen assembled with Solomon bared the role to be offered to manifest and fill the temple with God's glory. The wisdom of Solomon having learned from so many before him understood the death to glory ratio. Solomon understood it so much that he offered an innumerable ratio of death offering that he might receive an immeasurable amount of God's glory to fill the temple.

Let us consider my earlier point about an eighty thousand seat football stadium filled with believers for a Christian conference. A combination of eighty thousand sheep and oxen gathered together with no miracles taking place. We have to question why is that? Because today's sheep and oxen don't assemble with an offering mindset. They are assembled to receive and be given like a baby waiting on milk. Without an offering mindset we are milk Christians only good for receiving and lack understanding of how to sacrifice and offer to usher in the glory, presence and power of God into our assemblies.

Hebrews 5:12

12) For everyone that useth milk is unskillful in the word of righteousness: for he is a babe.

Ok so let's say death offering which is a direct parallel of fasting is a bit difficult for you as a believer. This would lead me directly to the next point I highlighted at the beginning of this chapter found in 2nd Chronicles 5: 13 , in which they offered one accord thanks giving and specifically worded praise.

Hebrews 13: 15

15) By him therefore let us offer the sacrifice of praise to God continually that is, the fruit of our lips giving thanks to his name.

Here in Hebrews 13:15 the word of God instructs us to offer the sacrifice of praise and thanks continually which we read that Solomon and his congregation did, which combined with the great death offering they found themselves in a cloud of God's glory.

A study of the one accord offering of thanksgiving and praise they offered, can help us identify another area that we of today's church are operating deficiently in. In order to do this let us take a look at the mindset of many believers attending service during praise and worship songs. Many believers believe the choir and or worship leader is there to sing to them or entertain them. I've personally been inside many church assemblies where three or four people stand and sing along with the worship leader.

Psalms 47: 7

7) .... : sing ye praises with understanding.

Psalms 22: 3

3) But thou art holy , O thou that inhabitest the praises of Israel.

I will use these two Psalms to illustrate the point of the need to sing praise with the understanding that God inhabits praise. Once we fully understand and embrace that God inhabits praise , then it has to become clear that praise offering is needed collectively from each and every believer in attendance at a particular service in order to usher in as much of God's glory and inhabiting presence as possible.

I personally once was in a prayer meeting with five other brothers. We lifted up each of the written prayer requests that had been submitted by our congregation. The prayer group usually was held for 1 hour so we had ten to fifteen minutes remaining before we were to leave so we used the time to sings praises. I was the worship leader of the church so I led my brothers in a few songs. Me and four of the other brothers stood and sang, while the sixth brother remained seated and sang with us. Halfway into the second song the sixth brother joined us in standing and a powerful wind of God's presence entered the room that is almost hard to describe. After leaving the prayer meeting I spent hours astonished on what we had experienced. Later that evening the Lord spoke to me and revealed that there's a heightened level of his glory that will inhabit when we praise him on total one accord. This means not some choosing to sit while others stand , or some choosing not to stand etc as if it's all optional. We must understand that the primary need for all in attendance is God, we are all there because we need God and desire to meet and fellowship with God. Because of this it behooves us to take every faith measure and exhibit whatever offering mindset ushers in God's cloud and glory.

Imagine if at the next Christian mega conference seating thousands. we all attended with an offering mindset , with many offering the death offering of a fast and "ALL" attending offering one accord praise. Imagine the cloud of Glory that would descend and the healings , miracles and yoke destroying that would take place. The great part is that not only can we imagine it but we also have the ability to actually do it, and not only at the mega conference but also at our weekly services.

So whether at the next Christian mega conference in your area or simply the next Sunday service at your home church , challenge yourself to adopt the offering mindset because it could most assuredly determine who you're there to see. No one believes or looks at it like they are attending to see the speaker , but unwillingness to offer could very well limit your experience to hearing the speaker and never seeing God's glory.

Hearing from God and seeing God's glory are not the same.

1ˢᵗ Thessalonians 1: 5

5) For our gospel came not unto you in word only, but also in power, and in the Holy Ghost, and in much assurance;

The gospel preached every Sunday often comes in word only, primarily because the people don't offer anything on behalf of the service and come strictly to receive. Let's be clear if I stand in front of a congregation to preach and read only one verse from the Bible to them, and then close the Bible and leave, they have heard from God because I've spoken from his living word. Hearing from God in such a limited capacity as reading one verse then leaving, would disappoint and probably upset the whole congregation as they file out to exit. It's indeed true that they had heard from God so then why would they be upset? Obviously they'd be upset because they expect more. Expecting more than that, is indeed a good thing, but I say why not expect it all, as far as his glory, power and miracles to be present each service. Expectation such as these can only be realized when the believers planning to attend have the offering mindset and exhibit willingness to offer on behalf of the house of God. Remember that it is whatsoever we loose on earth that he will loose from Heaven.

Matthew 16:19

And I will give unto thee the keys of the kingdom of heaven; ………………:
and whatsoever thou shalt loose on earth shall be loosed in heaven

It is time like never before to understand the magnitude of being given the keys to the Kingdom of heaven. A short summary of this fact is that we have the ability to open, loose, release and unleash the miraculous presence, glory and power of God.

Notes

Chapter 5

Answered by fire

2nd Chronicles 5: 6 , 13 , 14

6) Also king Solomon , and all the congregation of Israel that were assembled unto him before the ark , sacrificed sheep and oxen , which could not be told nor numbered for multitude.

13) It came even to pass , as the trumpeters and singers were as one , to make one sound to be heard in praising and thanking the LORD ; and when they lifted up their voice with the trumpets and cymbals and instruments of music , and praised the LORD , saying , For he is good ; for his mercy endureth for ever: that then the house was filled with a cloud ,even the house of the Lord;

14) So that the priests could not stand to minister by reason of the cloud: for the glory of the Lord had filled the house of God.

Before making my next series of points I will first offer a brief recap of points I raised to begin Chapter 4 concerning the offerings of King Solomon and his congregation of God's beloved people. Taking a second look at 2nd Chronicles chapter 5 verses 6, 13 and 14, first we see them sacrifice an innumerable amount of death offerings, followed by a one accord offering of praise and giving of thanks. Finally we see God respond to their offerings by appearing among them in a cloud of his powerful glory.

2nd Chronicles 6: 1

1) Then said Solomon, The Lord hath said......

2nd Chronicles 7: 1 - 3

1) Now when Solomon had made an end of praying, the fire came down from heaven, and consumed the burnt offering and the sacrifices; and the glory of the Lord filled the house.

2) And the priests could not enter into the house of the Lord, because the glory of the Lord had filled the Lord's house.

3) And when all the children of Israel saw how the fire came down, and the glory of the Lord upon the house, they bowed themselves with their faces to the ground upon the pavement, and worshipped, and praised the Lord, saying, For he is good for his mercy endureth for ever.

2nd Chronicles chapter 6 picks up the chain of events after Solomon and the group sacrifice death offerings, then thanks and praise offerings followed by the cloud of God's glory appearing, Solomon then lifts up a lengthy prayer that covers the entire chapter 6 so I only listed the beginning portion of verse 1 to serve as abbreviation for the prayer.

2nd Chronicles chapter 7 verse 1 tells us "now Solomon made an end of praying" indicating the end of his chapter 6 prayer. After offering up prayer in the midst of the cloud of God's glory an immediate answering from God by fire occurred leaving the people in astonishment and amazement indicated in verses 2 and 3.

All these events are amazing to read about, but more importantly , what can we learn and apply from these things. Combining a large collective of death offerings combined with a large collective of praise and thanksgiving offering loosed a mass cloud of God's glory upon the house of God which directly indicates that their sacrificial faith acts magnified God's presence in their midst. While God's magnified cloud of glory was in their midst the prayer of the leader was immediately and miraculously answered by fire for the whole congregation to experience and witness.

I've clearly outlined a faith formula and pattern, of death and other offerings equating to measures of God's glory and power in my book project The

Death to Glory Ratio Part 1 and now here in The Death to Glory Ratio Part 2. I've shown how men of God throughout all ages have used the same faith formula and calculations to net miraculous results.

Mark 9: 28 -29

28) And when he was come into the house, his disciples asked him privately, Why could not we cast him out?

29) And he said unto them, This kind can come forth by nothing, but by prayer and fasting.

When God establishes a means by which something must be done it is utterly foolish to try to go about accomplishing it any other way. It is indicated throughout scripture, and I've listed and highlighted many examples in Part 1 and Part 2 Death to Glory Ratio book series of God's presence being ushered in by believers willing to sacrifice and offer.

In the New Testament, our bodies represent the living sacrifice that bares the responsibility to offer the acceptable sacrifices that usher in the miraculous presence and glory of God.

Romans 8: 36

36) As it is written , For thy sake we are killed all the day long; we are accounted as sheep for the slaughter.

It must be recognized and understood that all the talk of death is spiritual talk in most instances and is not speaking in terms of literally dying, but instead is speaking in terms of offering our bodies in the likeness of death such as fasting.

Mark chapter 9 tells a story of a man with an ill and infirmed son who is bound by evil spirits. The man gets his son to Jesus and gets him healed and delivered, confessing to the Lord that he previously brought his son to the disciples who couldn't heal him. I pick the story up in Mark 9: 28 -29 where the disciples ask Jesus why they were unable to cast him out. Jesus answers the disciples "this kind can come forth BY NOTHING BUT PRAYER AND FASTING".

Scripture does not offer us a listing of every sickness, disease or physical infirmity that exists today nor all the physical or mental health problems caused by individual being under the bondage of evil spirits. This makes it impossible for us to know beforehand which miraculous healings will require us to fast. That being said, if your seeking healing for someone who's life is on the line due to illness why not calculate that a fast is needed to get the healing done.

We choose not to fast for the healing then when no healing occurs we lie on God and say it wasn't God's will to heal them as we watch them suffer or perish.

Matthew 17: 15- 17

15) Lord have mercy on my son; for he is a lunatic ,and sore vexed : for ofttimes he falleth into the fire , and oft into the water.

16) And I brought him to thy disciples, and they could not cure him.

17) Then Jesus answered and said , O faithless and perverse generation

Matthew chapter 17 and Mark chapter 9 both share the story of this man seeking healing for his son. Matthew 17 illustrates a point in Jesus' response to being told his disciples couldn't get the job done found here in Matthew 17: 17 where he calls them faithless for their inability. In Mark 9: 29

Jesus tells his disciple that healing and power such as this can come forth " BY NOTHING BUT PRAYER AND FASTING" and for lack of doing what had to be done here in Matthew 15: 17 he calls those particular disciples " FAITHLESS". Reading into the combined message of the two verses I summarize that not completing a faith task such as a healing when there is a clear means to do so is considered faithless to the Lord. Good for us that all these examples are put here for us to learn and grow from.

Mark 9: 29 stating that this kind can only come forth by prayer and fasting isn't put in the Bible to be overlooked or ignored in terms of the necessity of fasting to manifest miraculous healing.

Notes

Chapter 6

Applicable Wisdom and Revelation from Nehemiah

Nehemiah 13: 11-12

11) Then contended I with the rulers, and said, Why is the house of God forsaken? And I gathered them together, and set them in there place.

12) Then brought all Judah the tithe of corn and the new wine and the oil unto the treasuries.

Nehemiah was used by God to lead and accomplish great works for the Lord. One thing he was used for, was to lead others into the rebuilding and repair of the wall of Jerusalem. After 52 days the wall was completed and then Nehemiah gave two faithful men charge over the city.

As Nehemiah continued to seek the welfare of repairing Jerusalem, brings us to the verses that I opened this chapter with. Along with the rest of Jerusalem, the house of God was also completely destroyed by the Babylonia armies for Israel's long standing defiance and disobedience to the Lord. Now that Nehemiah is present at Jerusalem repairing, Nehemiah 13:11 shows us Nehemiah taking concern for the forsaken state of the house of God. After assembling and positioning rulers on the matter, verse 12 then tells us that all Judah brought tithes of corn , new wine and oil to the treasuries concerning the matter.

I want to focus attention and share divine revelation on the offerings they chose to bring to the treasuries concerning no longer forsaking the downtrodden state of the house of God that was in their midst. They offered Corn , New Wine and Oil.

Oil is often used throughout the Bible, especially the Old Testament as a literal and symbolic representation of the anointing and Holy Spirit. My first published book " The Supply of the Spirit of Jesus Christ and the Mystery of the Olive Branch dives very deeply into divine revelation of how Oil crushed and squeezed from Olives symbolizes anointing and Holy Spirit squeezed and crushed from believers.

Hosea 2:22

22) And the earth shall hear the corn, and the wine, and the oil ;

As Bible readers and students, it is important to understand that there are levels of Bible wisdom, knowledge and understanding. Through diligent study and fasting we can receive divine revelation. As believers from all over the world, we usually all have a language we read or write in and can usually obtain a Bible printed in our language. It does not necessarily require divine revelation or interpretation to understand what's plainly written in the language and writing that we comprehend. That is the milk level of the word of God.

Hebrews 5:13

13) For every one that useth milk is unskillful in the word of righteousness: for he is a babe.

    Divine revelation and interpretation unlocks Bible mystery and instruction into how to operate skillfully and miraculously in our faith so it's highly important to seek these levels. Once a believer begins to receive divine revelation, connections will become easier to recognize as to how what's literally being read often has a far greater figurative and symbolic meaning. A challenging aspect to all this then becomes explaining these things to babes and other believers which is exactly what I endeavor to do in each

and every one of my book projects
including the one you are reading.

Hosea 2:22

**22) And the earth hear the corn, and
the wine, and the oil;**

Reading this verse Hosea 2:22 in
any human language or writing does not
make sense in a literal sense. People do
not hear corn, wine or oil. Corn, oil and
wine are not sounds, so that point alone
should quicken understanding that corn,
oil and wine here in this verse is being
used to speak figuratively or symbolically
of something else. Corn, Oil and Wine
are all used at certain different places in
scripture symbolically to represent the

Holy Spirit and anointing. It's very important to note and remember that the Holy Spirit and the word of God are and operate as one. Understanding all these points we can then interpret the revelation we see found in Hosea 2:22 concerning the earth hearing the corn, oil and wine which symbolizes anointed word of God.

1st Timothy 5: 17- 18

17) Let the elders that rule well be counted worthy of double honour, especially they who labour in the word and doctrine.

18) For the scripture saith, Thou shalt not muzzle the ox that treadeth out the corn.

Here in 1st Timothy 5: 17 -18 points are mentioned about elders laboring and being considered worthy of reward, and this notion being compared to ox treading out corn. Timothy shows us a parallel and comparison of elders to ox and what they are treading out is corn which symbolizes anointing and word of God.

Matthew 9: 14, 15 and 17

14) Then came to him the disciples of John , saying , Why do we and the Phar'i-sees fast oft , but thy disciples fast not?

15) And Jesus said unto them, Can the children of the bridechamber mourn , as long as the bridegroom is with them? but the days will come , when the

*bridegroom shall be taken from them,
and then shall they fast.*

*17) Neither do men put new wine into
old bottles : else the bottles break, and
the wine runneth out, and the bottles
perish: but they put new wine into new
bottles and both are preserved.*

We see here in this segment
Matthew chapter 9 the term "New
Wine" being mentioned. Jesus is asked a
question about why his disciples haven't
been fasting. Jesus explains that they
will not fast while he is still on earth
with them, but once he is risen and
departed they will then fast. Jesus is
connecting fasting as purposeful in filling
bottles with new wine. Obviously there
are many more points and details that
can be extracted from these verses I've

listed from Matthew. But a summary of the points I want to use in order to stay on topic are fasting equating to filling bottles with new wine which are symbolic points to teach us.

I titled this chapter "Applicable Wisdom and Revelation from Nehemiah", because we can learn from the choice of things the people of God brought forth to be used in restoration, repair and rebuild of the house of God. Oil, Corn and New wine. The major component of the anointing oil of the Old Testament used to anoint the tabernacle was olives to crush and squeeze oil from, oxen were often yoked together to tread out corn and Jesus speaks of fasting putting new wine into bottles.

The first responsibility that
Nehemiah laid on the shoulders of the
people to raise the house of God out of
ruin was to bring and keep in store
mass quantities of anointing and Holy
Spirit. We as believers today are
responsible to tread out, squeeze out
and fast out mass quantities of anointing
into our churches and the world itself
that the yoke destroying and miraculous
signs wonders, healing and deliverance
powers of God will again be present as
they were in Bible times.

Notes

Made in the USA
Middletown, DE
28 June 2025

77446457R00038